Sermon Outlines for Special Days

Sermon Outlines for Special Days

Croft M. Pentz

Baker Book House
Grand Rapids, Michigan

Copyright © 1979 by Baker Books
a division of Baker Book House Company
P.O. Box 6287, Grand Rapids, MI 49516-6287

ISBN: 0-8010-7046-5

Sixteenth printing, March 2002

Printed in the United States of America

For information about academic books, resources for
Christian leaders, and all new releases available from
Baker Book House, visit our web site:
http://www.bakerbooks.com

CONTENTS

Sermon Outlines for Special Days

1

HAPPY NEW YEAR

"For a great door . . . is opened unto me" (I Cor. 16:9).

The New Year presents many opportunities. It is a time to evaluate our performance in the previous year. No one can be satisfied without knowing and having Christ in their life. All phases of Christ's life are a source of joy for the Christian. (1) His birth—the promised Messiah came. (2) His life—He healed and helped all. (3) His death—He paid for all man's sins. (4) His resurrection—He overcame death. (5) His ascension—He promised to return for His people. To be happy is very simple—have Christ and you have happiness.

I. **HAPPINESS THROUGH FELLOWSHIP**
   A. Fellowship with Christ (I John 1:7). Note the power of this fellowship—it cleanses us from all sin. This means that if we live according to Christ's words His blood cleanses us from all sin.
   B. Fellowship with Christians (Ps. 133:1-3). It is good for God's people to have fellowship and to live in unity. The Bible tells of having fellowship with the wrong type of people (II Cor. 6:17).
   C. Fellowship through the church (Ps. 122:1). Church attendance is important, especially as the coming of Christ draws near (Heb. 10:25).

II. HAPPINESS THROUGH FIGHTING

The Christian faces a battle (Eph. 6:12-18). If we don't fight we will be defeated. We must go forward and fight against the powers of the devil.

A. Fight sin (I Tim. 4:1-3). There will be sin in the new year, which we must fight. Since Satan knows his time is short, he will fight against us, seeking to destroy us.

B. Fight slackness (Matt. 24:12). Because of sin the love of many people becomes cold and indifferent. When a person becomes slack, or indifferent, he displeases God.

C. Fight sensuality (I Cor. 10:13). Satan will tempt you in every way. However, for every temptation there is strength to overcome.

D. Fight slothfulness (Rom. 12:11). There is no excuse for laziness in the life of a Christian. Lazy people get into trouble. Satan often works through lazy people.

III. HAPPINESS THROUGH FOLLOWING

A. Follow God's call (Matt. 4:19). If we follow God He will make us what He wants us to be.

B. Follow God's command (Matt. 22:37, 39). This requires complete love for God.

C. Follow God's commission (John 15:16). This involves witnessing and winning souls.

D. Follow God's character (I Peter 1:16). Be holy like God.

Happiness comes with salvation. However, we must maintain this happiness. How can we keep this happiness? (1) Read the Bible daily. (2) Take time to pray daily. (3) Always think the best of all people. (4) Always look on the good side of life. (5) Accept everything that comes into your life as a gift from God.

2

THE CHRISTIAN AND MUSIC

Ephesians 5:19

Martin Luther said, "Satan feared my songs more than my preaching." There are two types of Christian songs. (1) Hymns. These are songs about or to the Lord. (2) Gospel songs. These are songs of praise or worship. The Psalms were used as songs. There is much emphasis on singing in the Bible. Songs are usually divided into these areas: (1) songs of praise, (2) songs of worship, and (3) songs of prayer. The Bible tells of the stars singing together (Job 38:7). Ezra tells of a choir (Ezra 2:65). The psalmist tells of the various instruments used in singing to the Lord (Ps. 150:1–6).

I. **HEAVENLY SINGING**
   A. Come before the presence of the Lord with singing (Ps. 100:2). This is an excellent way to approach the Lord.
   B. God has put a new song within our heart (Ps. 40:3). This new song comes at the time of conversion.
   C. The Lord is my song (Exod. 15:2). This could be changed to "God has put a song in my heart."
   D. Paul and Silas sang praise to the Lord while they were in prison for preaching the gospel (Acts 16:25).
   E. Sing aloud to the Lord (Ps. 81:1).
   F. Sing thanks to the Lord (Ps. 92:1). All things take on new meaning when you sing praise to the Lord.

G. Sing with a joyful noise to the Lord (Ps. 95:2).

II. HAPPY SINGING

A. If we are happy we should sing (James 5:13). Happiness comes only through knowing God personally (Ps. 16:11).
B. We should make a joyful noise unto the Lord, who is the rock of our salvation (Ps. 95:1).
C. The children of Israel rejoiced when the Lord led them through the Red Sea (Exod. 15:1).
D. Having God within us causes us to sing praise and spiritual songs to the Lord (Col. 3:16).

III. HOPEFUL SINGING

A. The Israelites sang upon completing the temple (Ezra 3:10). They now had a place to worship. They had hope.
B. We must sing as long as we have our being (Ps. 104:33).
C. We should sing hymns and psalms unto the Lord (Eph. 5:19).
D. We can spread the name of the Lord through singing (Heb. 2:12). People will see our happiness and want what we have.
E. We will sing a new song in heaven (Rev. 14:2). If we cannot sing on earth, how will we sing in heaven?

A happy person will sing. One of the best ways of praising the Lord is through song. Singing is not only praise, worship, and prayer, it is also dedication and determination to serve the Lord. Singing praises changes the whole attitude of man. You cannot sing and complain at the same time. Singing will not only help you have victory over sin, Satan, and self, it will also help you keep the victory.

3

DEATH

John 14:1-3, Psalm 23:1-6, John 11:25, 26

THE CHRISTIAN DEATH
A.   Prepared death. We are prepared to meet God and to be in heaven.
B.   Peaceful death. We have no fear of the future.
C.   Profitable death. We will be with God forever.
D.   Precious death. God welcomes His children home.

THE PARADOX OF DEATH
A.   It brings sorrow, yet we know our loved ones are with Christ.
B.   It creates loneliness, but God comforts and fills the empty place with His presence.
C.   It creates misunderstanding, yet we know the Lord does all things well.
D.   It creates pain, but God heals the broken heart.

Death is powerful but cannot destroy memories. Therefore, think on the good times we had before death separated us.

I.   HOPE IN DEATH
A.   The house (II Cor. 5:1). The body is the house in which the soul lives.
B.   The help (Ps. 23:4). We have no fear because Christ is with us.
C.   The hope (I John 3:2). We will see Christ and be like Him.

D. The happiness (John 14:1-3). We have the promise of heaven.

II. HAPPINESS IN DEATH
A. Conversion (II Cor. 5:8). The soul absent from the body is with the Lord.
B. Comfort (Rev. 21:4). The "no mores" of heaven:
1) No more tears.
2) No more death.
3) No more sorrow.
4) No more pain.
5) No more darkness.

III. HELP IN DEATH
A. Promise (Deut. 33:27). His everlasting arms help and comfort us.
B. Power (John 11:25, 26). Though our body dies our souls will live eternally.
C. Peace (Matt. 5:4). Those who mourn will be comforted by the Lord.

Death is coming to all people (Heb. 9:27). Therefore, we must prepare for death. How does one prepare?
1) Admit you are a sinner (Rom. 3:23).
2) Believe in Christ as your Savior (Acts 16:31; Rom. 10:9, 10).
3) Confess your sins (I John 1:9).

Death comes suddenly (Prov. 27:1). Therefore, prepare for death today (II Cor. 6:2). Accept Christ as Savior and enjoy eternal life with Christ (John 3:16).

4

CHRISTIAN CONCERN AND COMPASSION

Matthew 9:36

Man is a sinner by birth (Rom. 3:23). If he remains a sinner, he cannot see God (John 3:1-8). The Bible says all who call upon the Lord will be saved (Rom. 10:13). However, man cannot be saved if: (1) He does not know *how* to call. (2) He does not know *where* to call. (3) He does not know *why* to call. (4) He does not know *when* to call.

I. THE CONFUSED CROWD

"But when he saw the multitudes." There were all types of people in the crowd that followed Christ.

    A.   Sick people. All types of people were healed by Christ (Matt. 8:16). Christ not only came to save man, but to heal man spiritually, physically, and mentally.

    B.   Sinful people (Rom. 3:23). All men are sinners. This is why our Lord came (Matt. 9:13). He didn't come to condemn but to convert; not to rebuke but to redeem.

    C.   Sorrowful people (John 8:3-11). Jesus forgives the woman guilty of adultery. God forgives all sin (I John 1:7).

    D.   Suffering people (Matt. 8:1-4). A leper is healed by Christ. Christ took time for all people.

    E.   Sad people (Luke 19:1-8). Zacchaeus was hated by many, yet Christ took time to see him.

II. THE COMPASSIONATE CHRIST

"He was moved with compassion on them."

    A.   Divine compassion (John 3:16). God was willing to give His only Son for the sins of mankind.

B. Dedicated compassion (John 10:18). Christ had power to give or to withhold His life.

C. Desirous compassion (II Peter 3:9). It is not the Lord's will that any perish, but that all be saved (Rom. 5:8).

D. Determined compassion (Matt. 26:39). Christ prayed, "Not my will but thine be done." Though it meant suffering, He was willing to pay the full price for our salvation.

III. THE CONCERNED CHRIST

"Because they fainted, and were scattered abroad, as sheep having no shepherd."

A. Helpless—"fainted." *No spiritual help.* Many cry out with David in Psalm 142:4. The ethiopian eunuch said to Philip,"How can I understand unless someone guide me?" (Acts 8:31).

B. Homeless—"scattered." *No spiritual hope.* The Philippian jailer did not know the plan of salvation (Acts 16:30, 31).

C. Hopeless—"no shepherd." *No shepherd to help.* Paul says, "How shall they hear without a preacher?" (Rom. 10:14).

How deep is your love for God? Note the fourfold question in Romans 10:14, 15.

A. How shall they *call* on Him in whom they have not *believed?*

B. How shall they *believe* in Him of whom they have not *heard?*

C. How shall they *hear* without a *preacher?*

D. How shall they *preach* except they be *sent?*

Do you have this compassion? Compassion is more than feeling sorry! Compassion is loving someone enough to help!

5

RESPECT FOR GOD'S DAY

Exodus 20:8–11

God gives man six days every week. All He asks is that man give Him one day per week. Some feel that one hour per week is too much for God. Man has 365 days a year; God asks for just 52!

I. **SABBATH (vv. 8–9)**
   A. Rest (Gen. 2:2, 3). God created the earth in six days, and took the seventh day as a rest day.
   B. Respect. God took a day for rest and refreshment. We should do the same. This shows respect for God and respect for our bodies.
   C. Righteous (v. 11). God hallowed this day.

II. **SUNDAY**
   A. Resurrection (Mark 16:2–9). Jesus rose from the dead on Sunday. It is called the Lord's Day.
   B. Respect (Acts 20:7). The early church worshiped on Sunday. They did not worship on the Sabbath.
   C. Reminder (I Cor. 16:2). Give your tithes/offerings on the

first day of the week. John called it the Lord's day (Rev. 1:10). Nothing is said of the Sabbath.

    D. Rejection (Col. 2:16, 17). These Jewish laws, such as keeping the Sabbath, were no longer in effect after Christ's resurrection.

Note Jesus' words: "And I, the Messiah, have authority even to decide what men can do on Sabbath days!" (Mark 2:28 LB).

III. SACRED

    A. Desire (Heb. 10:25). We desire a two-fold fellowship: (1) fellowship with God, and (2) fellowship with Christians. A Christian needs both of these, and they are found only in the church.

    B. Delight (Ps. 122:1). Christians are glad to attend the house of God for two reasons: (1) for the happiness received, and (2) for the hope received.

    C. Dedication (Luke 24:53). They were always in the temple. They enjoyed worshiping God. The church came first in their lives.

Note the importance of Sunday in the Bible. (1) Five times Christ appeared—each on Sunday. (2) The Holy Spirit descended on the disciples on Sunday. (3) The Lord's Supper was celebrated on Sunday. (4) Offerings were given on Sunday. (5) John was on the Isle of Patmos on Sunday. Sunday is God's day—keep it holy.

6

RESPECT FOR MARRIAGE

Exodus 20:14

Marriage is sacred! Marriage is for as long as the couple lives. Many books, movies, and magazines make a mockery of marriage. They encourage adultery and premarital sex. Sex outside of marriage is sin. If man repents God forgives the sin of adultery. However, it is a sin that man never forgets. In America we have about one million divorces annually.

I. **THE PREPARATION FOR MARRIAGE**
   A. Prepare mentally. Maturity is a must. A marriage is not on a trial basis (Mark 10:9). Not only do you make the vows to each other, you make them to God. He will hold you responsible.
   B. Prepare spiritually (Amos 3:3). Both people should be of the same faith.
   C. Prepare financially (I Tim. 5:8). It's a shame and a sin to marry and bring children that you cannot support into the world.

II. **THE PLAN FOR MARRIAGE**
   A. Sharing (Gen. 2:18-23). Man could not live alone so God created a woman. Marriage brings two people together and makes them *one!*
   B. Surrender (Gen. 2:24). Both husband and wife work as a team. "Me," "mine," and "my" become "ours."
   C. Submission (Eph. 5:22-24). Wives should submit to their husbands.

D. Showing (Eph. 5:25-32). Love your wife as you love yourself. The wife should respect the husband.

III. THE PRACTICE IN MARRIAGE
   A. Control (I Cor. 13:5). Real love will overlook mistakes and failures. Read the entire chapter from *The Living Bible*.
   B. Cooperation (Amos 3:3). The husband and wife must agree and work together. They should sit down and discuss differences without anger.
   C. Character (Eph. 5:23). The husband is the head of the house. To be an effective leader the husband needs wisdom from God.
   D. Conflicts. Talk things over. Learn to "give and take."

IV. THE PROBLEMS IN MARRIAGE
   A. The attitudes. (1) Lack of love, (2) lack of trust, (3) lack of respect, and (4) lack of understanding will cause problems in marriage.
   B. The Adultery
      1) Start—begins with lust (Matt. 5:27-28). Adultery begins in the heart.
      2) Scars (I Sam. 12:1-9). God forgives, but man suffers from guilt.
      3) Sorrow (I Cor. 6:9). Adulterers who do not repent cannot enter heaven. Those committing adultery destroy their souls (Prov. 6:32).
   C. The answer (Eph. 5:33). Stay in love after marriage.

In marriage the "we" comes before the "I." A couple was married for sixty years. When asked the reason for their successful marriage, the wife said, "I fell in love often." She paused, then said, "With the same man." Remember, love + trust + prayer + understanding will make any marriage a success. Marriage can be heaven on earth, but you must work at it—and don't forget to ask God for help.

7

THE MEANING OF FAITH

Hebrews 11:1-3, 6

What is faith? It is believing in God even though you have not seen Him. It is making the impossible become possible. Faith accepts God's Word and does not doubt. Faith is trusting God to divide the Red Sea; it is trusting God to make the walls of Jericho fall. Faith is building an ark before it rained; it is walking on the water when Christ says, "Come." It is being willing to offer your son as a sacrifice. Faith does not ask questions, it does not make excuses.

I. THE PROOF OF FAITH (v. 1).
   A.   Promise—"Now faith is the substance (Promise) of things hoped for." Consider these Old Testament promises:
      1)   Promise of pardon (Gen. 3:15; Isa. 53).
      2)   Promise of prayer (Jer. 33:3).
      3)   Promise of provision (Exod. 15:26).
      4)   Promise of peace (Isa. 26:3).
   B.   Proof—"The evidence of things not seen." Faith believes before it sees. See Hebrews 11—great men of the Bible had complete faith in God.

II. THE PEOPLE OF FAITH (v. 2)
   "Men of God in days of old were famous for their faith" (LB).
   A.   Faith in God during problems (Heb. 11:8-10). Abraham faced many problems, but was successful because of his faith.

B. Faith in God during pain.
1) Faith (Job 1:1–21). Job lost all he had, yet he did not complain.
2) Firm (Job 13:15). God could slay him and Job would still not question His leading.
3) Faith (Job 19:25). Job knew that God was alive.
4) Faithful (Job 42:12, 13). In the end Job was rewarded for his faith.
C. Faith in God during prayer (I Kings 18:25–41).
D. Faith in God during persecution (Dan. 6:10–28).

III. **THE POWER OF FAITH (v. 3)**
A. The Creator (Gen. 1:1). God created the world.
B. The creation (John 1:3). All was made from nothing.
C. The control (Col. 1:16). God not only created all things, but He also controls all things.

IV. **THE PRACTICE OF FAITH (v. 6)**
A. Pleasure—"But without faith it is impossible to please Him."
B. Person—"For he that cometh to God must believe that he is." He is God and these are His attributes: (a) all powerful, (b) knows all things, (c) present in all places at the same time.
C. Promise—"And that he is a rewarder of them that diligently seek him." (Note Jer. 29:16).

If we trust God we will have faith for the future. If we cannot trust God for small things, we will not trust Him for large things. Faith and doubt never go together. Faith sees the answer; it does not look at the circumstances.

8

GOD'S CALL TO YOUTH

"Don't let anyone think little of you because you are young. Be their ideal; let them follow the way you teach and live; be a pattern for them in your love, your faith, and your clean thoughts" (I Timothy 4:12, LB).

Our young people are seeking a leader. They are searching for someone who will give them a sense of direction. God is calling them; the only question is will they answer His call. It is the same call given in Matthew 4:19.

I. **THE CALL TO SEPARATION**
   A. Places of sin (I John 2:15-17). Don't love the world.
   B. People of sin (II Cor. 6:17). Your friends influence you.
   C. Practices of sin (I Tim. 5:22). Keep yourself pure!
   D. Purity from sin (I Thess. 5:22). Stay away from what's wrong.
   E. Purging from sin (II Cor. 7:1). Cleanse yourself!
   F. Playing with sin (Prov. 6:27, 28). Sin always leaves marks.
   G. Power of sin (Rom. 12:2). Don't join with the world.

II. **THE CALL TO SURRENDER**
   A. Time (Ps. 90:12). Never waste your time. Include God in all you do (Eccles. 12:1).
   B. Talk (James 1:19; 1:26). Every time you open your mouth, you show what is in your heart.
   C. Thoughts (Prov. 23:7). You are what you think. We should have the mind of Christ (Phil. 2:5).

III. THE CALL TO SACRIFICE

Note the words of Jesus in Luke 9:23.

A. Decision—"If any man will come after me." There is a choice.

B. Denial—"Let him deny himself" (cf. Gal. 2:20).

C. Dedication—"And take up his cross daily."

D. Determination—"And follow me" (see Matt. 4:19).

IV. THE CALL TO STAND

A. Purpose (Dan. 1:8). We must make a decision to live for God. Sixty-nine years after Daniel "purposed" to live for God he was freed from the den of lions.

B. Power (Dan. 3:24–27). Christ stood with the three Hebrew boys.

C. Problem (Mark 8:36–38). If we are ashamed of Christ, He will be ashamed of us.

V. THE CALL TO SERVICE

A. Worship (John 4:34). We serve Him by attending church, reading the Bible, and praying.

B. Work (Eccles. 9:10). We serve Him by putting our heart into what we do.

C. Witnessing (Acts 1:8). We serve Him by telling others about God and His love.

God is calling today. Do you hear His voice? Are you living close enough to Christ that you *can* hear His voice? Sometimes we become spiritually deaf. Sometimes we don't hear His voice because we don't care! Open your heart and allow Him to speak to you.

9

THE DEATH OF CHRIST

Christ was born to die. Without His blood there could be no forgiveness of sin (Heb. 9:22). Christ the perfect Son of God became the Lamb of God.

I. THE PROMISE OF HIS DEATH

He would come through "the seed of the woman." He would destroy the works of sin and Satan (Gen. 3:15).

II. THE PROPHECY OF HIS DEATH

He would suffer and die for our sins. He would suffer physically as well as mentally (Isa. 53; Ps. 22).

III. THE PAIN OF HIS DEATH

No one could measure the pain He endured. No one could know what it meant for Him to be separated from: (1) His followers, (2) His family, (3) His friends, (4) His Father.

IV. **THE PLACE OF HIS DEATH**
Calvary means the place of the skull. They tried to make Jesus look as guilty as possible (see Luke 23:33).
V. **THE PERSON IN HIS DEATH**
If we accept Jesus as king we will not have to face Him as judge (Rev. 20:11-15).
VI. **THE POWER IN HIS DEATH**
The most important words in His death were, "It is finished." He did not mean His life was finished. He meant that the plan of salvation was now completed (see John 19:30).
VII. **THE PARDON IN HIS DEATH**
His death provides forgiveness from all sin (I John 1:9; 1:7). He forgave a thief on the cross (Luke 23:42, 43).

The death of Christ is in vain unless we accept His pardon. Note the words of John 3:16. We must believe with both our minds and our hearts (Rom. 10:9, 10). Man is born a sinner (Rom. 3:23). He should pay for his sin by being punished (Rom. 6:23). But Christ suffered for us and forgives all sin (Ps. 103:3).

10 ✓

THE RISEN CHRIST

John 11:25, 26

The greatest words to man are—*Christ Is Risen!* Many thought death was the end of Christ and His ministry. However, He rose from the dead as He promised. Forty days after His resurrection He ascended into heaven (Acts 1:11).

I. THE PERSON

"I am the resurrection and the life."

A. Salvation (II Corinthians 5:17). With salvation comes a complete change in our outlook.

B. Sustainer. Not only does he save us from sin He keeps us from falling away from Him (I Peter 1:5; Jude 24; II Tim. 1:12).

II. THE PLAN

"He that believeth in me."—Man must believe in his heart (Rom. 10:9, 10). When he does this he will practice the teachings of Christ.

A. Practice by having faith (Heb. 11:1). Though we can't see God we must believe in Him (Heb. 11:6). Increase your faith (Rom. 10:17).

B. Practice by being faithful. The Bible warns us to be faithful until death (Rev. 2:10).

C. Practice by fellowship. We must have fellowship with the Lord as well as with one another (I John 1:7).

III. THE PROMISE

"Though he were dead, yet shall he live."

A. A life of happiness (Ps. 16:11). Happiness can be achieved only by being satisfied. Man cannot be satisfied until he knows Christ.

B. A life of hope (Rom. 6:23). Though the wages of sin is death, God's gift is eternal life. Death is not the end to the Christian—it's the start of eternal life.

IV. THE POWER

"And whosoever liveth and believeth in me shall never die."

A. The provision (Isa. 53:5). Christ's death brought life to mankind.

B. The promise (John 5:24). By believing in Christ we pass from death to life. Faith in Christ means we will not stand with the condemned at judgment (Rev. 20:11-15).

C. The plan (Isa. 55:7). Man must be willing to abandon wickedness and trust in Christ.

We often sing, "You ask me how I know He lives? He lives within my heart." When He lives within us we will have peace (John 14:27). We will have a peaceful mind (Phil. 4:7). When Christ is with us we need not be afraid (Ps. 23:43).

11

LIFE-CHANGING WORDS

Graduation is not the end—it's the beginning! Now is the time to put into practice what you have learned. How well you can apply what you have learned will determine your future success.

I. WORK

It was said that Thomas A. Edison worked twenty hours a day. Edison said, "Show me a satisfied person and I'll show you a failure." Note the words of Solomon (Eccles. 9:10).

II. STUDY

President Lincoln said, "I will study, then when the opportunity comes, I will be ready." Knowing how to read but not reading is no different than the person who cannot read. Note the words of warning from Paul (II Tim. 2:15).

III. LOVE

Christ told us to love Him (Matt. 22:3). As we love Him we will love others (Matt. 22:39). There must be a love for: (1) God, (2) parents, and (3) church. Love will cause us to: (1) respect, (2) obey, (3) honor, and (4) be faithful.

IV. CONVERSATION

God gave man two ears but only one mouth. He made the ears

to remain open but the mouth to close. We will be judged by our words. Each time we open our mouths, we show what's in our hearts.

V. PRAYER

One cannot be a success without remembering God. Note the words of Solomon (Eccles. 12:1). Prayer changes things, people, and circumstances. Note the words of Jesus in Matthew 7:7-9).

VI. GIVING

Life is not what we get but what we give. The Bible says it is more blessed to give than to receive (Acts 20:35). Give your time and talent to help others.

VII. FAITH

Helen Keller, though deaf and blind, did wonders because of her faith in God as well as in herself. Note the words of Philippians 4:13.

Practice these words daily in your life, and you will be a success in all you do. Most people never plan to fail—they fail to plan. You cannot be a success by hoping and wishing. It will take hard work, study, and applying these words to your life.

12

THE POWER OF PENTECOST

Acts 17:6

The results of Pentecost not only changed the church world but the secular world as well. In the thirty-two years after Pentecost the whole world heard about Christ. They did not have printing presses or church buildings. The same power that changed Peter from a reed to a rock changed others. In turn they changed their world. Note three things that these people had: (1) the Spirit (2) determination, and (3) willingness to work.

I. THE CHANGING POWER

    A. Personalities changed (II Cor. 5:17). This brings a change in attitude, actions, and ambition. Note the words in Ezekiel 36:26. If a man's heart is changed his personality will change.

    B. Purpose changed. After the conversion they were dedicated to a life of service. They went from house to house (Acts 5:42).

    C. Practices changed (Acts 8:1-3; 9:1-6). Paul (Saul) was transformed from a persecutor to a preacher. "At once Saul began to preach in the Jewish places of worship that Jesus is the Son of God" (Acts 9:20, NLT).

II. THE COMPASSIONATE POWER

Note Paul's compassion (Acts 20:31). Compassion is more than love. It is love that acts. It is love that does something!

    A. Compassion that grows (Acts 20:31). Paul watched over the Christians for three years.

    B. Compassion that gives (Acts 21:13). He was ready to give his life for Christ.

C. Compassion that goes (Mark 16:1). He obeyed God's command.

III. THE CONVERTING POWER

To convert means "to change."

A. Conversion from a life of sin (Acts 2:41). Here 3,000 are converted. Some of these had helped to crucify Christ.

B. Conversion from the power of Satan (Acts 19:19). The evil books were destroyed and the power of Satan was broken (I John 4:4).

C. Conversion from a life of slavery (Acts 15:1-20). We are no longer under the law but are now under grace.

IV. THE CONTINUING POWER

"And they were faithful in listening to the teaching of the missionaries" (Acts 2:42, NLT).

A. What did the apostles teach?
1) Salvation (Acts 16:31; Acts 4:12). There is only one way to salvation.
2) Surrender (Acts 26:19). Do not be disobedient to the heavenly vision.
3) Suffering (Acts 5:41). Be happy to suffer for the sake of the gospel.
4) Sacrifice (Acts 15:26). They risked their lives for the gospel.

B. God has given us the Holy Spirit for a purpose—to advance the kingdom of God. Note the power He has given us:
1) Power to preach (Acts 1:8). This includes the power to witness and win others.
2) Power to perceive the means of advancing His work (I Cor. 12).
3) Power to practice the fruits of the Spirit (Gal. 5:22, 23).

13

REMEMBERING

Joshua 4:1 -8

One of man's greatest failures is forgetting God's blessings. The children of Israel often did not give thanks for God's gracious presence. Despite the miracles which God performed, they could only complain about the hardships and privations of the wilderness.

I. REMEMBER PAST DECISIONS

   A. Moses (Heb. 11:25). Moses had to make a choice. He could have continued to live among the rich, but instead he chose to live with God's people. As the result God made him a leader. He was the man who would receive the Ten Commandments.

   B. Joshua (Josh. 24:15). Joshua challenged the people to make a choice. He then made a choice for himself and his family.

   C. Solomon (I Kings 3:9). Solomon could have asked for anything, but he asked for wisdom.

II. REMEMBER PAST DEDICATIONS

   A. Daniel (Dan. 1:8). Daniel's dedication strengthened him for the time when he would face the den of lions (Dan. 6:1 -24). Dedication kept him from "following the crowd."

B. Hebrew boys (Dan. 3:9-29). Three Hebrew boys were willing to take a stand for God instead of bowing to the golden image. Though it meant the fiery furnace, they were dedicated enough to spend time in the fire for the Lord.

C. Paul (Acts 20:24). Nothing could make Paul give up. He suffered so much for the Lord (II Cor. 11:24-28). All sufferings he bore were the result of a dedicated life.

III. REMEMBER PAST DOCTRINE

We could list many doctrines of the past that are being changed today by many liberal churches. Here are just a few:

A. Pardon (Isa. 53:5; Rom. 10:13; John 3:16).
B. Peace (Isa. 26:3; John 14:27; Phil. 4:7).
C. Punishment (Ps. 9:17; Mark 16:16).
D. Promise (John 14:1-6; I Thess. 4:13-18).
E. Prayer (Jer. 33:3; Eph. 3:20).

We enjoy Christianity today because many were willing to give their lives. The prophets, apostles, and early Christians gave their lives for the sake of the gospel. Hebrews 11:36-38 mentions the many who suffered for what we have today. God has not asked that we die for Him (though we may be asked to do so). He asks that we live for Him.

14

WOMEN OF THE BIBLE

"Who can find a virtuous woman? for her price is far above rubies" (Prov. 31:10). After creation God saw that Adam was lonely and created a companion for him (Gen. 2:18). Note: it is not good for man to be alone (Gen. 2:21-23). When a man takes a wife they become "one flesh" (Gen. 2:24). Let's look at some of the women of the Bible.

    A.   Lot's wife (Gen. 19:26). She loved sinful Sodom more than the commands of God. Because of this she was lost.

    B.   Potiphar's wife (Gen. 39:7-14, 20). She tempted Joseph. When he refused to give in she lied, and Joseph was sent to prison.

    C.   Jezebel (I Kings 21:1-16). She encouraged her husband Ahab to have Naboth killed so that he could take his vineyard. She also persecuted Elijah. She died a terrible death.

    D.   Delilah (Judg. 16:4, 20). Delilah was paid to trick Samson.

    E.   Herod's wife (Mark 6:21-28). Herod stole his brother's wife. John exposed this sin. Because of the advice of Herod's wife John was beheaded.

II. SACRED WOMEN

    A.   Sarah (Gen. 21:1-8). Sarah was over ninety years old. Yet God gave her a son, Isaac. She is mentioned in the "Bible Hall of Fame" (Heb. 11:11). She is called "the mother of nations."

B. Hannah (I Sam. 1:5-28). After many years of waiting God gave her a son. His name was Samuel.
C. Samson's mother (Judg. 13:1-25). God gave her a son to deliver Israel.
D. Elisabeth (Luke 1:13-25, 36-70). Her son became a great preacher. He was known as John the Baptist, who introduced Jesus as the Lamb of God.

III. **SERVING WOMEN**
A. Bathsheba (I Kings 2:13). Though she was guilty of adultery her son, Solomon, became the wisest man that ever lived.
B. Mary (Luke 1:26-55). An angel appeared to Mary and told her that she would be the mother of Jesus. This was a fulfillment of Isaiah 7:14.
C. Mary of Bethany. She sat at the feet of Jesus: (1) for instruction (Luke 10:39), (2) for comfort (John 11:32), (3) for service (John 12:3).
D. Dorcas (Acts 9:36-41). Note: "full of good works and almsdeeds." Salvation should produce good works.
E. Eunice (II Tim. 1:5). She left a lasting impression on Timothy.

Women have much to do in controlling the course of the world. Many women "work behind the scenes" in making the home and community a success. Women are also becoming involved in many other areas of the employment scene. God created woman to be a help to man. As you read the Bible you will see that God's plan for woman is to help and encourage man.

15

THE CHRISTIAN WIFE

Proverbs 31:10-31

"If you can find a truly good wife, she is worth more than precious gems!" (Prov. 31:10, LB). A man may be the head of the home, but the wife is the heart. Behind all successful men are women. A wife can help her husband by standing by him and encouraging him. Some wives are so busy trying to make a good man out of their husband that they have no time to be a good wife.

I. **A CHRISTIAN WIFE HAS CHRISTIAN MATURITY**
   A. Her attitude—"You wives must submit to your husbands' leadership in the same way you submit to the Lord" (Eph. 5:22, LB).
   B. Her actions—"Their wives must be thoughtful, not heavy drinkers, not gossipers, but faithful in everything they do" (I Tim. 3:11, LB).
   C. Her acceptance (Eph. 5:23). God's plan is for the husband to be the head of the home.

II. **A CHRISTIAN WIFE HAS CHRISTIAN MODESTY**
   A. Life of respect (I Peter 3:1). The wife respects her husband as the head of the home.

B. Life of restraint—"And the women should be the same way, quiet and sensible in manner and clothing. Christian women should be noticed for being kind and good, not for the way they fix their hair or because of their jewels or fancy clothes" (I Tim. 2:9, LB).

C. Life of righteousness (I Sam. 1:5–28). Hannah's dedication to the Lord has a great impact on her son, Samuel.

A Christian wife does not draw attention to herself. She dresses to please the Lord. Her husband and family are first. She sacrifices her time, life, and energy for others.

III. A CHRISTIAN WIFE HAS CHRISTIAN MANNERS

A. Her conversation—"Better to live in the desert than with a quarrelsome, complaining woman" (Prov. 21:19, LB).

B. Her character (Prov. 11:16). A good woman lives a good life and has good character.

C. Her control (Gal. 5:22, 23). The fruits of the Spirit are evident in her daily life.

A dedicated Christian wife has a great impact on the husband, children, and the world. A wife who rebels agains her husband rebels against God. There cannot be happiness in a home where the wife does not follow God's plan for her life.

16

THE CHRISTIAN HUSBAND

Ephesians 5:22–33

God created man in His image (Gen. 1:27). Man was made a living soul (Gen. 2:7). God saw that it was not good for man to live alone so He made a helper for him (Gen. 2:18). It is God's plan that Christian husbands be leaders in the home, church, and community. Our nation was founded by Christian men. God wants men who will put Christ first in their lives.

I. **THE CHRISTIAN HUSBAND IS A LEADER**
   He is the leader of the home (Eph. 5:23).
   A. This involves making decisions (Josh. 24:15). Joshua made a decision for his family. Of course, he did not make all the decisions on his own.
   B. Leadership involves discipline (Prov. 13:24). Children should be taught to obey.
   C. Training is more than teaching (Prov. 22:6). Training is getting people to practice what you teach.

II. **THE CHRISTIAN HUSBAND IS A LABORER**
   A. The price of work (Gen. 3:19). Man has to earn his living "by the sweat of his brow."

B. The provision of work (I Tim. 5:8). If a husband does not provide for his family, he is worse than a heathen.

C. The power of work (Eccles. 9:10). Whatever we do we should put our whole heart into it.

D. The plan for work (Rom. 12:11). Ambition is essential to the laborer. When you don't feel like it, work anyway.

III. **THE CHRISTIAN HUSBAND IS A LOVER**

A. A Divine love.

1) He loves God (Matt. 22:37). God is first in his life.

2) He loves the church (Ps. 122:1). He is faithful at all times.

3) He loves all people (Matt. 22:39). This takes God's help.

B. Domestic love.

1) His wife (Eph. 5:25, 28). He loves his wife as much as he loves himself.

2) His family (Eph. 6:4). He takes time with the children, teaching them to read, teaching them manners, and taking them to the park, etc. Love always gives. You may give without loving, but you cannot love without giving.

Many husbands don't want the responsibilities of being a husband and a father. As the result we have many problems. When a husband takes his rightful place in the home (Eph. 5:33), there will be a happy home.

17

GOD'S SEARCH FOR MEN

Ezekiel 22:30

God created man in His image (Gen. 1:26; 2:7). He was created for fellowship with God. Sin marred this fellowship, but God made a way to redeem man from his sin (Gen. 3:15). God would send Jesus into the world to die for the sins of man (Isa. 53:5). Through this man would be born again (John 3:1–8). After being born again man is called to do God's work (John 15:16; Mark 16:15). He does not call all to be ministers, or missionaries, but He does call all men to be soul-winners.

I.   **GOD LOOKS FOR DECISIVE MEN**
    A.   Joshua decided that he would serve God (Josh. 24:14).
    B.   Joshua decided that his family would serve God.
    The husband is the leader of the home (Eph. 5:23). Since he is the leader, he should be the spiritual leader.

II. **GOD LOOKS FOR MEN WITH DESIRE**
    A.   Desire to know the person of God (Phil. 3:10). Knowing God in a personal way (II Tim. 1:12).

B.   Desire to know the plan of God (Ps. 32:8). God will make His will known to us if we seek Him.
C.   Desire to know the power of God (I Peter 1:5). His power is available to keep us (I Peter 1:5). Note Paul's words about the power of God (Rom. 1:16).
D.   Desire to have the protection of God (Ps. 91). God is able to guide man through all times of trouble.

III. **GOD LOOKS FOR MEN WITH DEDICATION**
A.   Dedicated to serve God. It takes a strong person to serve God.
B.   Dedicated to stand for God. Anyone can quit; anyone can go along with the crowd. But to stand and be different is difficult and requires God's help (Phil. 4:13).
C.   Dedicated to suffer for the Lord. See II Timothy 3:12.

IV. **GOD LOOKS FOR MEN WITH DETERMINATION**
A.   Willing to suffer for the Lord as Paul suffered (Acts 20:24).
B.   Willing to allow Satan to persecute as Paul was persecuted.

God's work only goes forward as man does His work. God could use angels, but He depends on man. He worked through the judges, kings, prophets, disciples, apostles, and church leaders. He works through the laymen, who dedicate their lives to Him. *The greatest need in any church is dedicated laymen.*

18

THE CHRISTIAN CITIZEN

"Give it to Caesar if it is his, and give God everything that belongs to God" (Matt. 22:21, LB). "Remind your people to obey the government and its officers, and always to be obedient and ready for any honest work" (Titus 3:1, LB).

I. **RIGHTS OF A CITIZEN**
   A. Freedom to worship. All religions are protected by the Constitution. The churches are not taxed and contributions to the church are tax-deductible.
   B. Freedom of speech. We are permitted to say what we wish as long as we do not violate the rights of other citizens. We are permitted to disagree with the policy of our government.
   C. Freedom of the press. We are permitted to publish freely within certain legal limits. The church may publish gospel literature without interference from the government.

II. **RESPONSIBILITY OF A CITIZEN**
   A. Cooperation (Matt. 25:35-39). We should help those who are in need. The Christian doesn't just pity those in need—he helps them.

B. Concern (I John 3:17). One cannot love God without helping others. Love always acts. Real love will give and share.
C. Consecration (Ps. 122:1; Heb. 10:25). To the Christian citizen the church is first (Matt. 6:33).
D. Contribute (Luke 6:38). Give of your time, life, and money, and God will give back to you.

III. RESPECT OF A CITIZEN

A. Rules (I Peter 2:13, 14). We must obey the laws of the land. We may not agree with the laws, but God commands us to obey.
B. Rulers (I Peter 2:17). We should honor and respect our leaders. We respect their position.
C. Righteousness (Prov. 14:34). Righteousness exalts a nation. No nation can be great and remain great without the help of God.

President John F. Kennedy said, "Ask not what your country can do for you. Ask what you can do for your country." As a Christian citizen you can do much for your country. Here are some ways in which you may help your country. (1) Pray. Pray daily for the leaders and for the nation. (2) Vote. Every Christian should vote. (3) Encourage civic pride. It costs millions of dollars yearly to clean up litter. (4) Evangelize. Win the non-Christian to Christ.

19

LEISURE LIVING

With the passing years man has become more pleasure-minded. Resorts and motels are crowded and each year more are being built. There is nothing inherently wrong with enjoying life and leisure. It is only when the search for pleasure begins to interfere with our responsibilities as Christian laborers that leisure time can be a problem.

I. CALL TO LEISURE

    A. Rest (Gen. 2:1-3). God worked six days and rested one. Today man works five days and rests two.

    B. Relaxation (Mark 6:31). Jesus told the disciples to take a vacation.

    C. Respect (I Cor. 6:19). Our bodies are the temples of the Holy Spirit. Therefore, we should take good care of our bodies.

II. CONDEMNATION OF LEISURE

    A. Selfish leisure (Gal. 5:24). Desires and ambitions must be put aside. Christ must be first (Matt. 6:33).

    B. Sensual leisure (Luke 12:19). Note these words, which are so true of many today—". . . take thine ease, eat, drink, and be merry." In other words, have a good time. Don't worry about tomorrow.

C. Shameful leisure (Luke 8:14). Jesus spoke of a seed falling among thorns, "And that which fell among thorns are they, which, when they have heard, go forth, and are choked with cares and riches and *pleasures of this life,* and bring no fruit to perfection."

D. Sorrowful leisure (Eccles. 12:1). Solomon, who knew God but gave himself to pleasure, found that in the end there was no lasting joy.

E. Separating pleasure (Luke 12:20). The rich farmer had pleasure but lost his soul!

III. **CONSECRATION OF LEISURE**

It is important that we dedicate our whole being to God.

A. Consecrated plans (Prov. 3:5, 6). Always allow Christ to be first in your plans. Put the church and God before your personal plans.

B. Pleasures (Ps. 16:11). Christ will show us what real pleasure there is in serving God and living for Him.

C. Person (Gal. 2:20). We must be willing to give up our selfish plans, desires, and ambitions.

Jesus taught that we must deny ourselves (Luke 9:23). Paul tells us not to be conformed to this world (Rom. 12:2). This means not to follow the people, practices, and pleasures of the world. As Christians we must be different. Pleasure must never come between us and God. "No man can serve two masters" (Matt. 6:24).

20

RESPECT FOR PARENTS

Exodus 20:12

A Chinese man traveled in America for six months. When asked what impressed him most about America, he answered, "The way parents obey their children." In many homes the father is not the head—just a figurehead. Disobedience at home will lead to disobedience in the school and disrespect for authority. Children should be taught and even forced to obey parents. You cannot begin too early to teach this important lesson.

I. THE PRECEPT

"Honor your father and mother" (Exod. 20:12).

    A.   Love your parents (Col. 3:20). Show your love by obeying them.

    B.   Obey your parents (Eph. 6:1). Obey always—not only when you agree with your parents.

    C.   Respect your parents (Prov. 1:8). Listen to their advice.

    D.   Honor your parents (Matt. 15:4). The Jews put a child who disobeyed the parents to death.

    E.   Defend your parents. Always defend your parents.

    F.   Thank your parents. Thank them for all they have done for you.

II. THE PARENTS
A. Provision by parents (I Tim. 5:8). The first duty of parents is to provide food, clothing, and shelter.
B. Practices of parents.
  1) Teach (Deut. 6:7). Teach manners, respect, and fear of God.
  2) Train (Prov. 22:6). A good example will have an impact on them.
  3) Temper (Eph. 6:4). Never punish in anger. Don't nag; be a good example at all times.
C. Punishment by parents.
  1) Control (Prov. 22:15). Correction drives out foolishness.
  2) Chastise (Prov. 19:18). Correct the child while there is hope.
  3) Correct (Prov. 13:24). Don't withold correction.

III. THE PROMISE
A. Reward—"That thy days may be long upon the land which the Lord thy God giveth thee" (Exod. 20:12).
B. Reaping (Gal. 6:7). What we sow, we will reap. In many instances parents get no more respect from their children than they deserve. Respect must be earned.

(1) Disobedience, (2) disrespect, and (3) distrust are three ways in which children rebel. Unless these are checked in the early years of the child's life, there will be problems ahead. Someone once said, *"There is no such thing as bad children. There are just bad parents."*

21

THE CHANGED LIFE

Ezekiel 36:26

Because man is born in sin (Rom. 3:23), he must be born again. Sin cannot enter heaven (Rom. 6:23). When man accepts Christ he is born again (John 3:1-8). He is made new in Christ. He has become the son of God (John 1:12). Man cannot change his life without Christ's help.

I. **NEW CREATURE (II Cor. 5:17)**
   A. New love (Matt. 22:37, 39). This love is from God.
   B. New life (Gal. 2:20). Christ is in us and we are in Christ.
   C. New longings (Phil. 3:10). Paul had one desire—to know Christ!
   D. New looking (I Thess. 4:13-18). Christians are looking for the return of Christ.

II. **NEW COMPANY**
   A. New father (John 1:12). Before we accepted Christ Satan was our father (John 8:44).
   B. New family (Matt. 23:8). We are brothers and sisters in the Lord.
   C. New friends (II Cor. 6:17). We abandon the world and live a different life.

III. **NEW CHARACTER**
   A. Actions (Gal. 5:16). We walk in the Spirit and are under the control of the Spirit.

B. Attitudes (Prov. 23:7). Our attitudes (thoughts and emotions) will control our life.

C. Ambitions (John 8:32). We strive to know Christ and His teachings.

D. Affections (I John 2:15-17). We don't love the world.

IV. NEW CONVERSATION

A. Thinking (Ps. 19:14). The goal is to have our every thought acceptable to Him.

B. Talking (Prov. 21:23). "Keep your mouth closed and you'll stay out of trouble" (LB).

C. Tale-bearing (Prov. 26:20). Gossiping always creates problems.

V. NEW CONTROL

A. Temper (James 1:19). We should be swift to hear, slow to speak.

B. Tongue (James 1:26). If we can't control our tongue our religion is in vain.

C. Temptation (I Cor. 10:13). God will provide the power to overcome temptation.

VI. NEW COMPASSION

A. Love for God (Matthew 6:33). Christ is first in our life.

B. Love for enemies (Matt. 5:44).

C. Love for the church (Ps. 122:1).

D. Love for the Bible (Ps. 119:11).

E. Love for prayer (I Thess. 5:17).

The Bible warns us to cleanse ourselves (II Cor. 7:1). As Christians we should abstain from all appearance of evil (I Thess. 5:22). We should keep ourselves pure (I Tim. 5:22).

22

GOD AND WORK

Proverbs 6:6 –11

God does not condone laziness—He condemns it! The apostle Paul tells us, "Not slothful in business; fervent in spirit" (Rom. 12:11). There are many who feel that the world owes them a living. No one can read the Bible without seeing the emphasis which is put on work. The foolish virgins were lazy and did not have enough oil for their lamps. Because of this they could not attend the wedding (Matt. 25:1–13). Jesus had very harsh words for the man who did not make his talent increase. He called the man a "wicked and slothful servant" (Matt. 25:26–30).

I. **THE REASON FOR WORK**
   A. God commenced it (Gen. 1:1). The first verse of the Bible shows how God worked in creating the earth. After God worked six days He rested from His work (Gen. 2:2).
   B. God commanded it.
      1) Sweat and work (Gen. 3:19). Having the government support you is not the way of the Bible.
      2) Scope of work (Exod. 20:9). Our nation was built by men who were willing to work long and hard hours.
   C. God commended it (Prov. 12:11). Hard work will provide us with bread. Also notice, "Plenty of bread" (Prov. 28:19). *God promises no loaves to the loafer.*

II. **THE REALM OF WORK**
   A. Working physically (Eccles. 9:10). Put your whole heart into what you do. "Do with all thy might."

1) Provision (I Tim. 5:8). A Christian provides for His family. A true Christian will not be lazy!
2) Profit (Prov. 14:23). There is personal profit in labor. We can be proud of doing a good job and earning an honest living.
3) Pleasure (II Thess. 3:12). There is pleasure in *earning* and *eating* our own bread.

B. Working mentally. Think for yourself. Have the courage to speak out for what you believe.
1) Spiritual thinking (Prov. 23:7).
2) Sacred thinking (Ps. 19:14).

C. Working spiritually. Jesus said that He had to work (John 9:4).
1) Seeking the sinners (Mark 16:15).
2) Showing the sinners (John 3:16).
3) Saving the sinners (James 5:20).

III. THE RESULTS OF WORK

A. Peace (I Thess. 4:11). Work destroys idleness. Idleness can cause trouble.
B. Plenty (II Thess. 3:10). If we do not work, then we should not eat!
C. Pleasure (II Thess. 3:8). Here Paul says that he did not eat *free bread.* Too many want to do just enough to "get by." This attitude is evident in our churches as well.

Salvation is not gained by works (Eph. 2:8, 9). However, salvation does produce good works. Solomon says of a good woman, "She works far into the night" (Prov. 31:18, LB). He also says she is never lazy (Prov. 31:27). Jesus said, "I have finished the work which thou gavest me to do" (John 17:4).

23

CHRISTIAN SOLDIERS

"Thou therefore endure hardness, as a good soldier of Jesus Christ" (II Tim. 2:3). Soldiers are very important to any country. Through their services our country has been defended. Countries enjoy peace and security because soldiers were willing to serve. The Bible compares Christians to soldiers.

I. **THE SOLDIER'S TASK**
   A. To follow. They follow the orders of their leaders. The Christian follows the orders of Christ. The soldier is forced to follow. The Christian follows by choice (Matt. 4:19).
   B. To fight. They fight to save our country. The Christian fights the good fight of faith (I Tim. 6:12). He fights against sin, temptation, and Satan.

II. **THE SOLDIER'S TRAINING**
   Note the words of Paul in II Timothy 2:3.
   A. Discipline. Just as a soldier needs discipline, so the Christian soldier needs self-control (II Cor. 9:24–27).
   B. Dedication. The soldier is dedicated to his work. God wants all Christians to have this same obedience (John 2:5).
   C. Denial. A soldier puts his country above everything else. Christ must be first in our lives (Matt. 6:33).

III. THE SOLDIER'S TOOLS

No soldier is sent to battle without proper tools. God has given His followers special "spiritual tools" to accomplish His work.

A. Spiritual tools (II Cor. 10:4). These spiritual tools destroy the works of Satan.

B. Special tools (Eph. 6:13-17). These tools protect us from attacks.

C. Successful tools (Eph. 6:18). Prayer is the most powerful tool we can use in this battle.

IV. THE SOLDIER'S TESTING

A. Physical testing. Paul had a thorn in his flesh (II Cor. 12:7-10). God wants strong soldiers so He tests us.

B. Mental testing. Satan uses doubt to destroy God's people. God wants us to trust Him fully (Phil. 4:7).

C. Spiritually tested. This is a battle against Satan (Eph. 6:13).

V. THE SOLDIER'S TRIUMPH

A soldier is welcomed home after a battle. Christ will welcome us home. He will honor us for our faithfulness (Rev. 2:10).

A. Fight—"I have fought a good fight" (II Tim. 4:7).

B. Finished—"I have finished my course" (II Tim. 4:7).

C. Faith—"I have kept the faith" (II Tim. 4:7).

D. Faithfulness (II Tim. 4:8). A crown awaits us!

A soldier who refuses to serve brings dishonor to country and family. A soldier who does not serve well also brings shame. A Christian who does not faithfully serve God brings shame to God as well as His work. However, the soldier who serves well brings honor to both his family and his country.

24

THANKSGIVING

Psalm 100

The Bible has much to say about thanksgiving. Note the number of times the word *thanks* or related words appear in the Bible: thanks—75, thanksgiving—28, thank—27, thankful—3, thanked—3, thanksgivings—2, thankfulness—1 (a total of 139). Thanksgiving is one of the most needed things in the church today. We have many prayer requests, but few who praise and thank the Lord.

I. **THE SOUND (v. 1)**
   A. Joyful praise—"Make a joyful noise unto the Lord" (cf. Ps. 9:11). Share His goodness with all people.
   B. Joyful people—"All ye lands." The psalmist says all those who have breath should praise the Lord (Ps. 150:6).

II. **THE SERVICE (v. 2a)**
   "Serve the Lord with gladness."
   A. Joy of salvation. He has brought us out of the pit of sin and has put a new song in our heart (Ps. 40:3).
   B. Joy knowing the Savior (Matt. 1:21). Jesus saves man from all sin!

III. **THE SINGING (v. 2b)**
   "Come before his presence with singing."
   A. Songs of praise. Even in prison Paul and Silas could sing praise unto God (Acts 16:25).

B. Song of pardon (Isa. 40:2, 3). Brought from the depths of sin we are given a new song.

IV. **THE SUPERNATURAL (v. 3a)**
A. Controller—"Know ye that the Lord he is God." All things are under His control (Col. 1:16).
B. Creator—"It is he that hath made us, and not we ourselves." God created man (Gen. 2:7). Because of sin God must re-create man at the time of salvation (II Cor. 5:17).

V. **THE SHEEP (v. 3b)**
A. Personal—"We are his people" (see John 1:12; 3:16).
B. Protection—"And the sheep of his pasture" (see Isa. 53:5).

VI. **THE SHOWING (v. 4)**
A. Praise—"Enter into his gates with thanksgiving, and into his courts with praise" (cf. I Thess. 5:18).
B. Worship—"Be thankful unto him, and bless his name" (cf. John 4:24).

VII. **THE SAMENESS (v. 5)**
Three things that remain the same with the Lord:
A. The Lord is *good* (Rom. 8:28).
B. His *mercy* is everlasting (Ps. 103:17).
C. His *truth* endures to all generations (John 8:32; 14:6).

How often do you thank the Lord? Being thankful changes our whole outlook. It changes our attitudes. A thankful person is a happy person. Nothing hurts God's work and His church more than a complaining Christian!

25

JESUS AND CHRISTMAS

Luke 2:7-14

Without Christ there would be no Christmas. Today the entire world pauses to remember the birth of this great man. The entire history of the world centers around the birth of Christ.

I. THE CRADLE
   A. Promised birth (Isa. 7:14; 9:6). His birth was promised 700 years in advance.
   B. Pure birth (Matt. 1:18, 23). Christ was born of a virgin. This was a miracle birth; it was a supernatural birth.
   C. Planned birth (Gen. 3:15). Adam and Eve received the first promise of the coming Christ—the Messiah. The prophet Micah told the town where Christ would be born (Mic. 5:2).

II. THE CONSECRATION
   A. To do God's will (Matt. 26:39). He never questioned God's will for His life. He willingly accepted the burden placed on him.

B. To God's Word (Isa. 53:10). God's Word prophesied of His suffering and death.

C. To God's way (Isa. 53:5). This was God's plan: Christ would pay the full price of salvation.

III. THE CROSS

A. Promised death (Isa. 53). His death was foretold more than 700 years in advance.

B. Purpose of death (Heb. 9:22). Without His blood there would be no forgiveness of sin.

C. Power of death (Luke 23:44, 45). Christ forgave a thief on the cross. Through His death He brought forgiveness to all men.

IV. THE CROWN

A. Crown of Christ (Heb. 10:12). Christ ascended into heaven and now sits at the right hand of God. Christ finished the work God gave Him to do.

B. Crown for Christians (II Tim. 4:8). This crown is for faithfulness in the Christian life. Note the words of Revelation 2:10 and Matthew 24:13.

Christ came into the world as a babe. During His stay on earth He taught us how to live and serve Him. He died, arose, and ascended into heaven. This babe who grew into a man will come again. This time He will return as the judge of all mankind.